To: ....

From: ....

My Life in Color

Designed by Christian Art Gifts

Images used under license from Shutterstock.com

Printed in China

ISBN 978-1-4321-1611-8

16 17 18 19 20 21 22 23 24 25 – 10 9 8 7 6 5 4 3 2 1

christian art gifts®

YOU ARE NEVER TOO OLD TO SET ANOTHER GOAL OR TO DREAM A NEW DREAM
- C. S. Lewis

LIFE

DOESN'T

HAVE TO BE

perfect

TO BE

WONDERFUL

HOW TO USE THIS *journal*

Embark on a journey of personal discovery that combines creativity with reflection and dreams with doodles in a faith-filled and fun way. Journaling and coloring are a wonderful combination as both allow you to slow down, be present in the moment and focus on the details.

Forget about to-do lists for a while; ignore the hustle and bustle around you and spend time focusing on the present. Allow God to speak to you as you reflect and create.

It doesn't matter how talented you are, this journal is your own personal expression of yourself. Use the prompts provided to spark an idea or a reflection and make this journal your own. You can doodle, stick, stamp, paint, cut and paste in these pages. Give your creativity free rein and remember, it doesn't have to be perfect to be beautiful!

LIFE
IS
art
Live
YOURS
IN
Color

Imagine spreading color in your world through the good deeds you do. Imagine every smile and kind word to be a splash of color. Think about ways you can show kindness, be a blessing and color your world.

"EVERY
artist
WAS
FIRST AN
AMATEUR."

RALPH WALDO EMERSON

Ephesians 2:10

We are God's masterpiece. He has created us anew in Christ Jesus, so we can do the good things He planned for us long ago.

My mission

My vision

CULTIVATE AN attitude OF gratitude

TODAY I'M *grateful* FOR:

Psalm 136:1

Give thanks to the LORD, for He is good. His love endures forever.

A page of good thoughts ...

Today
I CHOOSE
joy

YOU GET TO DETERMINE YOUR ATTITUDE.
EVEN WHEN THINGS ARE TOUGH,
YOU GET TO DECIDE HOW YOU WILL
RESPOND TO WHAT HAPPENS TO YOU.

THINK

ABOUT HOW YOU CAN HAVE
A POSITIVE ATTITUDE TODAY:

- ....
- ....
- ....
- ....
- ....
- ....
- ....
- ....

Psalm 118:24

This is the day the LORD has made. We will rejoice and be glad in it.

A DAY IN MY LIFE LOOKS LIKE THIS ...

A NEW
COMMAND
I GIVE
you:
LOVE
ONE
another
AS I HAVE LOVED
YOU

John 13:34

What message of love can you send today? Think of something you can do or say to someone who needs a little TLC.

- ....
- ....
- ....
- ....
- ....
- ....
- ....

I am a

little pencil

in the hand of

a writing *God*

who is sending a

love letter

to the world.

Mother Teresa

My Heavenly Father ...

Look up the Scriptures and write them down.

Loves me (John 3:16)

Forgives me (Psalm 103:12)

Cares for me (Matthew 11:28)

Redeems me (Job 19:25)

Delights in me (Zephaniah 3:17)

Cleanses me (1 John 1:9)

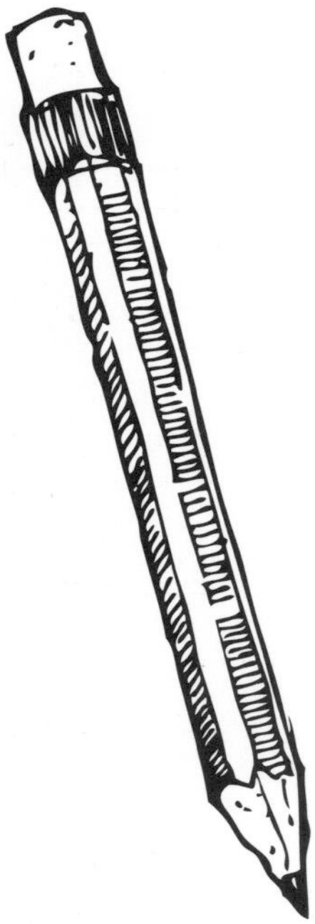

WRITE YOUR PLANS IN PENCIL AND GIVE GOD THE ERASER

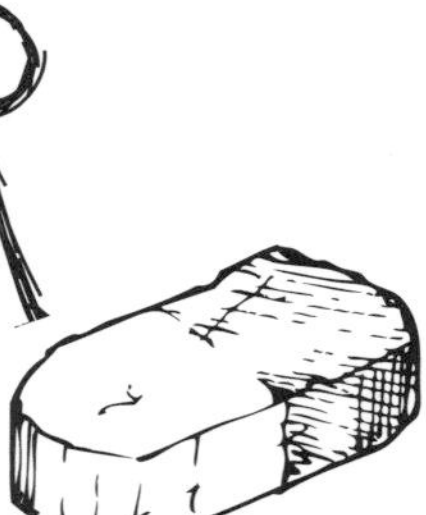

List any plans and dreams you have.

Ask God to show you what He wants you to do.

Be prepared to adapt your plans to His will. He might have even better things in store for you than you can imagine!

MY PLANS

MY DREAMS

Proverbs 16:9

In their hearts humans plan their course,
but the LORD establishes their steps.

LIFE WITHOUT GOD IS LIKE AN UNSHARPENED PENCIL IT HAS NO POINT

Areas I can simplify ...

IF YOU CAN'T BE A

PENCIL

TO WRITE ANYONE'S

happiness

THEN TRY TO BE A NICE

ERASER

TO REMOVE SOMEONE'S

sadness

Sometimes there is nothing you can do for a person who is suffering except to offer a shoulder to cry on and a listening ear. Just talking about something can make a person's pain seem a bit less. Who can you help today? Write out the following verses on kindness and compassion with your favorite pens:

COLOSSIANS 3:12

GALATIANS 5:22-23

EPHESIANS 4:32

FOR THESE I PRAY ...

USE WHAT
TALENTS
YOU
POSSESS...

The woods would be very silent if no birds sang there except those that sang best.
Henry van Dyke

List the talents that God has given you.
Remember that God can use you even though
you think your abilities are not good enough.
Is there any ministry that could use your talents?

- ....
- ....
- ....
- ....
- ....
- ....
- ....
- ....
- ....
- ....
- ....
- ....
- ....
- ....
- ....

Romans 12:6

We have different gifts, according to the grace given to each of us.

A letter to my future self

EACH

new day,

JUST LIKE
A CRISP

white page,

IS FILLED WITH POTENTIAL AND POSSIBILITY.

WHAT KIND OF STROKE WILL YOU MAKE ON YOUR PAGE TODAY? LET LOVE, KINDNESS, JOY AND PEACE COLOR YOUR LIFE.

Isaiah 1:18

"Though your sins are like scarlet,
they shall be as white as snow;
though they are red as crimson,
they shall be like wool."

PEOPLE IN MY LIFE
I'M GRATEFUL FOR:

David Nicholas

Step outside tonight and breathe in the expanse of the night sky. The same God who placed each of the stars in the sky cares about you and will lead you through the dark nights and difficult times in your life. Praise Him for His beautiful and magnificent creation and thank Him for being your Light in the darkest night.

Isaiah 40:26

Look up into the heavens. Who created all the stars? He brings them out like an army, one after another, calling each by its name. Because of His great power and incomparable strength, not a single one is missing.

MY PERSONAL ACCOMPLISHMENTS & ACHIEVEMENTS:

Broken
crayons
still color

For whatever personal reason, you might be feeling broken, miserable and like a failure. Just remember that whatever has happened in your past, God can still use you today. You can still fill the world with color in a way that only you can. Bring your thoughts and feelings to God today and give your brokenness to Him. He is gracious and forgiving.

Psalm 51:17

The sacrifice You desire is a broken spirit.
You will not reject a broken and repentant heart, O God.

God IS GRACIOUS & FORGIVING

HE
WILL COVER
YOU
WITH HIS
Feathers
& UNDER
HIS WINGS
YOU
WILL FIND
refuge

PSALM 91:4

MAKE
TODAY
great!

List a few ways you can take this day from average to awesome.

HINT:
Those who bring sunshine into the lives of others cannot keep it from themselves.

J. M. Barrie

TODAY
don't just
settle for
average
MAKE IT A
GREAT
fantastic
DAY

Psalm 96:1-2

Sing a new song to the LORD!
Let the whole earth sing to the LORD!
Sing to the LORD; praise His name.
Each day proclaim the good news
that He saves.

A PRAYER OF PRAISE & THANKSGIVING

FOR I CAN DO
EVERYTHING
THROUGH
CHRIST
WHO GIVES ME
STRENGTH

Philippians 4:13

WHEN WAS THE
LAST TIME
YOU
DID SOMETHING
FOR THE
FIRST TIME?

MY BUCKET LIST

Do ....

See ....

Cook ....

Explore ....

Go ....

Forget ....

Remember ....

Dream ....

Listen to ....

Pray ....

Plant ....

Write ....

Discover ....

Love ....

Surprise ....

Share ....

Walk in faith ....

Live ....

Experience ....

Draw ....

Fill ....

Allow ....

Renew ....

Give back ....

Be ....

Read ....

Eat ....

Play ....

Make ....

Ride ....

Create ....

Enjoy ....

Travel ....

Watch ....

Visit ....

Grow ....

The most important thing
on my life's to-do list

LIFE
IS LIKE A
RAINBOW
YOU NEED BOTH THE SUN
AND THE RAIN TO MAKE
ITS COLORS APPEAR.

SOMETIMES WE NEED A LITTLE RAIN IN OUR LIVES FOR US TO GROW CLOSER TO OUR HEAVENLY FATHER. REFLECT ON TIMES WHEN YOU'VE EXPERIENCED STORMS AND HOW YOU'VE GROWN THROUGH THEM.

Matthew 5:45

"Your Father in heaven causes His sun
to rise on the evil and the good, and sends
rain on the righteous and the unrighteous."

QUOTES THAT INSPIRE ME

ALWAYS
REMEMBER
YOU
ARE
loved

Today, just marvel at the wonderful
fact that your heavenly Father loves you!
Let your heart soar in praise to Him.

Romans 8:39

No power in the sky above or in the earth below - indeed, nothing in all creation will ever be able to separate us from the love of God that is revealed in Christ Jesus our Lord.

A LETTER TO MY LOVE

Three lessons to be learnt from a pencil:

1. Everything you do leaves a mark.
2. Pain always sharpens you.
3. It's what's inside that counts.

We can learn a wise lesson
from the humble pencil!
Think for a moment about how and
where you are leaving your mark today.

Micah 6:8

And what does the LORD require of you?
To act justly and to love mercy and to
walk humbly with your God.

Things I want to start doing ...

Even if I knew
that tomorrow the
world would go to pieces,
I would still plant my
apple tree.
Martin Luther

What can you do today that
will benefit the future generation?
What legacy do you want
to leave behind?

Psalm 150:6

Let everything that breathes sing praises to the LORD! Praise the LORD!

WAKE UP
EVERY
morning
WITH THE
THOUGHT
THAT SOMETHING
WONDERFUL
IS ABOUT TO
happen.

Our thoughts have a huge influence on the quality of our lives.
Be conscious of what you think about and choose God-honoring thoughts.
List some of the positive things you can think about, and what kind of thoughts to avoid.

FIX
YOUR
thoughts
ON WHAT IS
TRUE, AND
HONORABLE,
AND RIGHT, AND PURE,
AND LOVELY,
AND ADMIRABLE.
THINK
ABOUT THINGS
THAT ARE
excellent
AND WORTHY OF
praise.

PHILIPPIANS 4:8

WORRY
IS LIKE A
rocking
CHAIR
IT GIVES YOU
SOMETHING
TO DO
BUT IT
GETS
YOU
NOWHERE

Do you worry endlessly and needlessly?
In Matthew 6, Jesus tells us not to worry,
so bring all your worries to Him and lay
them at His feet. And leave them there.

relax • refresh • reconnect

Philippians 4:6–7

Don't worry about anything; instead, pray about everything. Tell God what you need, and thank Him for all He has done. Then you will experience God's peace, which exceeds anything we can understand. His peace will guard your hearts and minds as you live in Christ Jesus.

ANSWERED prayers

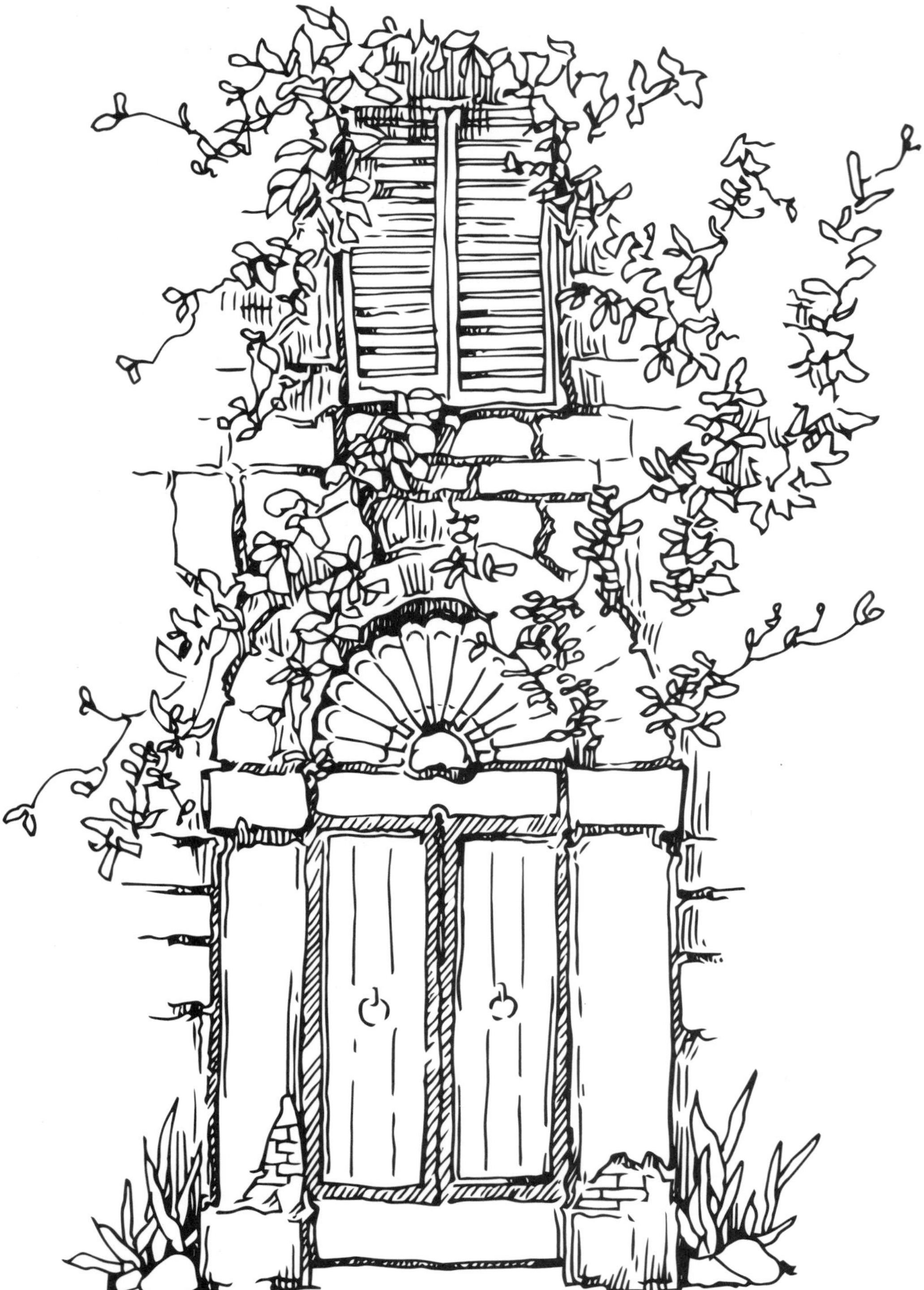

Bloom where God plants you!

Think about where you are in life right now.
God has placed you where you are for a reason.
In your home, your church and your work place,
you can bloom and bear fruit for Him.
Think about how you can show the fruit of
the Spirit in your life today.

Galatians 5:22-23

The fruit of the Spirit is love, joy, peace, forbearance, kindness, goodness, faithfulness, gentleness and self-control.

Bear fruit in every good work.

List the fruit of the Spirit and reflect on each one.

A smile
IS THE prettiest
thing you can
wear

The world is so focused on external beauty, but what counts to God is your character and how you treat others. Who needs a smile from you today?

- ....
- ....
- ....
- ....
- ....
- ....
- ....
- ....

Ask God to
help you
be the
person He
wants
you to be.
Be beautiful
on the inside.

1 Peter 3:4

You should clothe yourselves with the beauty that comes from within,
the unfading beauty of a gentle and quiet spirit, which is so precious to God.

CREATE
in Me a
CLEAN
Heart
O
God
PSALM 51:10

THE TIME
IS NOW!

What have you been putting off?

It might be a phone call you need to make or a letter you need to write. Whom do you need to tell that Jesus loves them and died to save them? There is no time like the present to do those things of eternal significance.

2 Corinthians 6:2

God says, "At just the right time, I heard you. On the day of salvation, I helped you." Indeed, the "right time" is now. Today is the day of salvation.

WRITE OUT

Jeremiah 29:11

Do something

TODAY

that your future self will

THANK

YOU for.

What could you start doing or stop doing that will make a difference in your life? Giving up bad habits will reap rewards and starting good habits will have life-long benefits. How about starting a Bible reading plan or attending a women's Bible study course or prayer group? Or how about attempting a healthy lifestyle change?

Colossians 3:23-24

Whatever you do, work at it with all your heart,
as working for the Lord, not for human masters, since you
know that you will receive an inheritance from the Lord
as a reward. It is the Lord Christ you are serving.

GROW IN FAITH
CREATE BEAUTY
INSPIRE OTHERS

Color and cut out the designs on the following pages.
Use them in the journal or in any way that inspires you.

FAITH
love
Believe
Joy
Grace
HOPE
BLESSING
PEACE

Joyful in HOPE

Trust IN THE Lord

Praise the Lord!

God is good!

Rejoice in TODAY

LIFE IS BEAUTIFUL